I0485602

Heart Designs Coloring Book

An adult coloring book for stress-relief, relaxation, meditation and creativity

By

S.B. Nozaz

Copyright © 2015 by S.B. Nozaz

All rights reserved worldwide. No part of this publication may be reproduced or distributed in any form or by any means, mechanical, electronic or stored in a retrieval or database system, without written permission from the copyright holder.

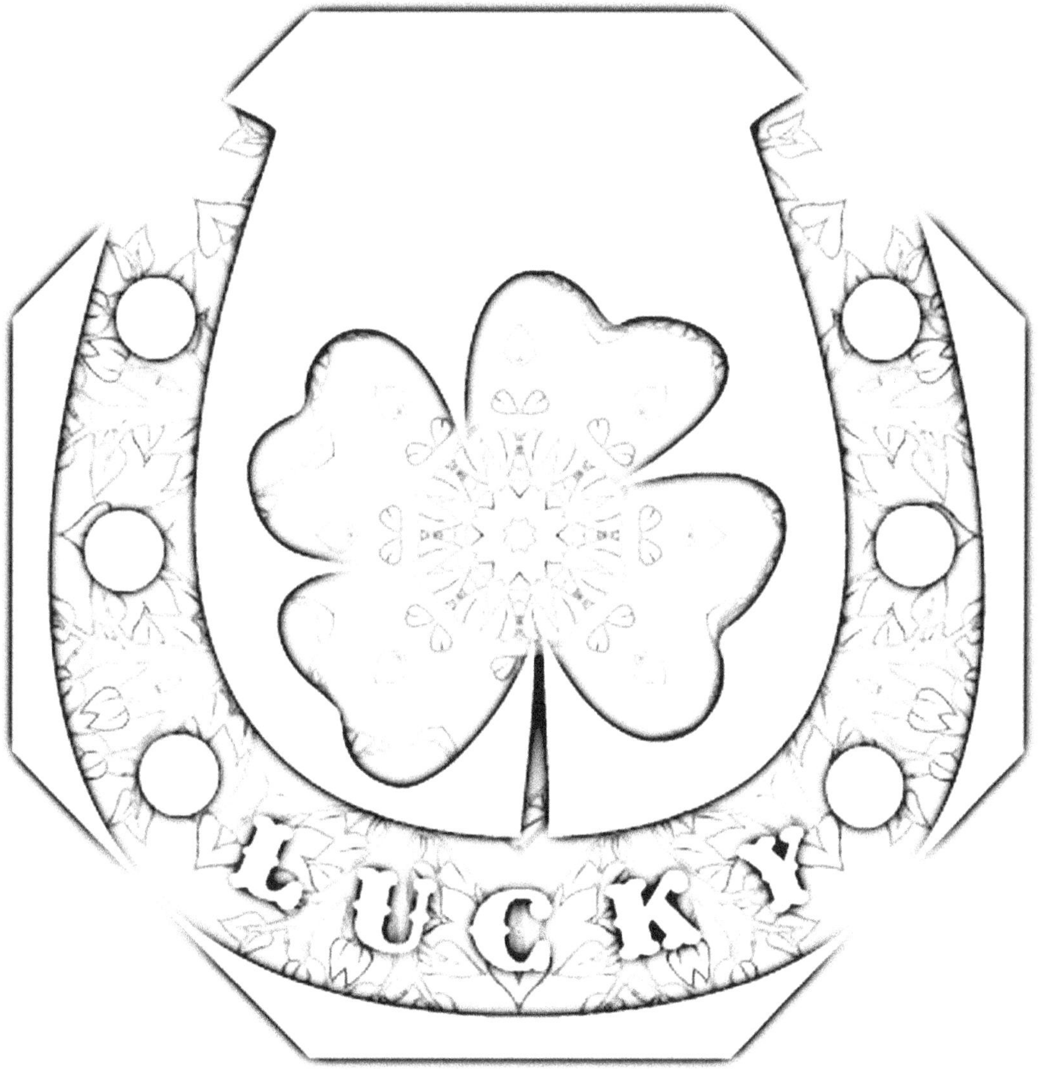
LUCKY

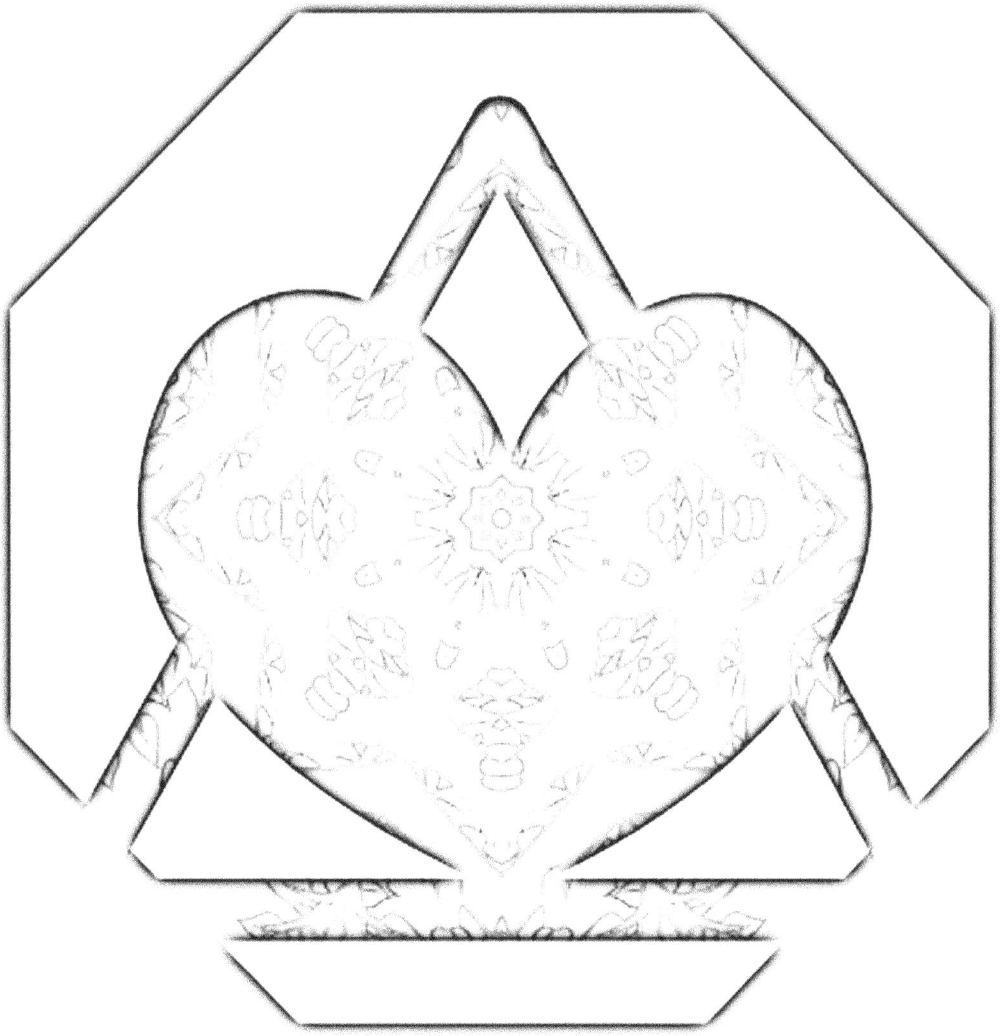

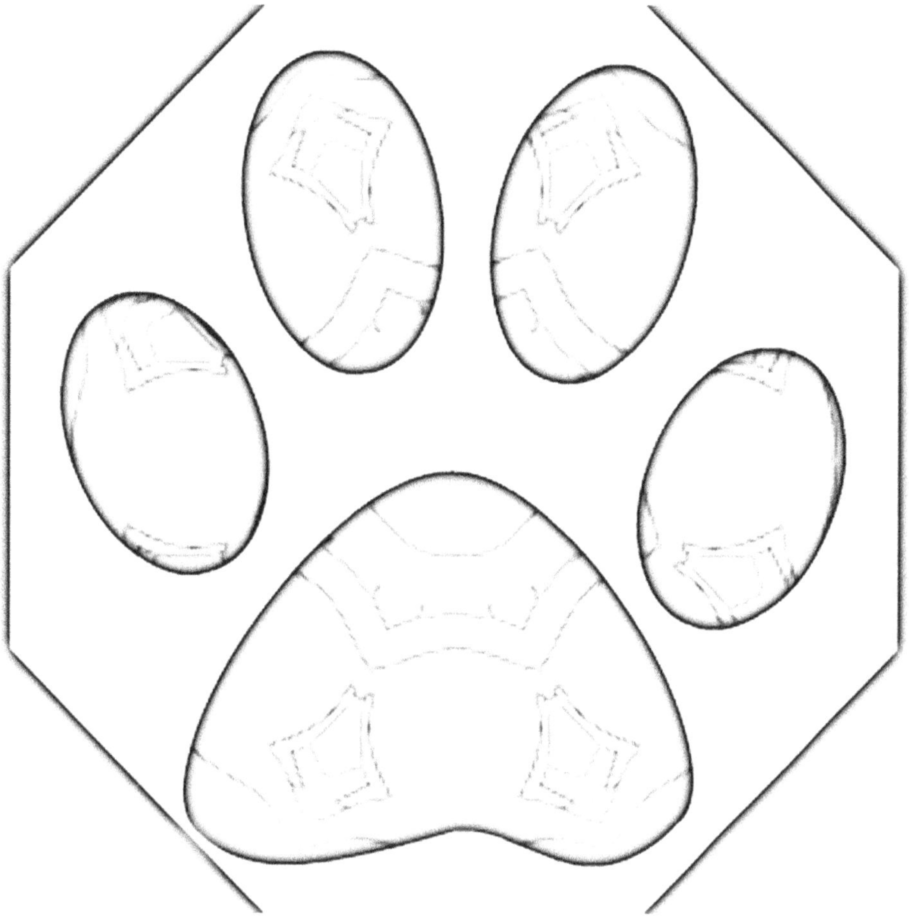

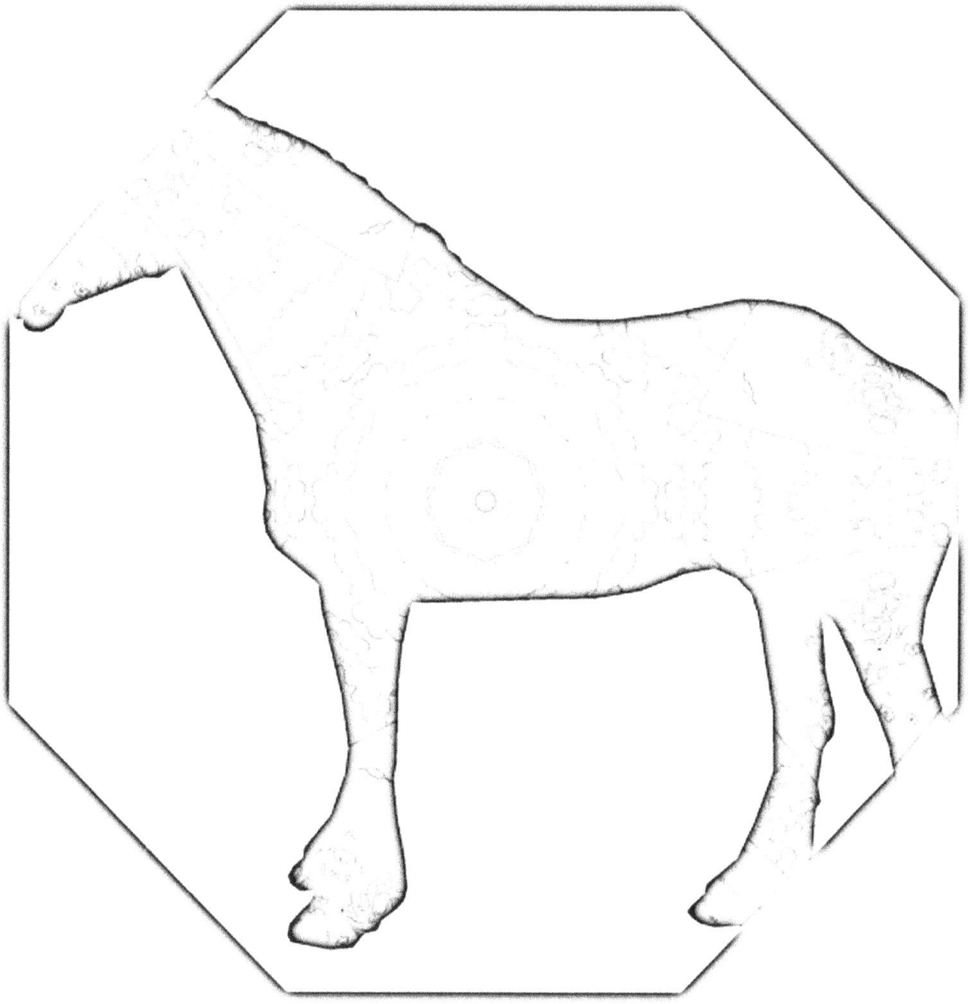

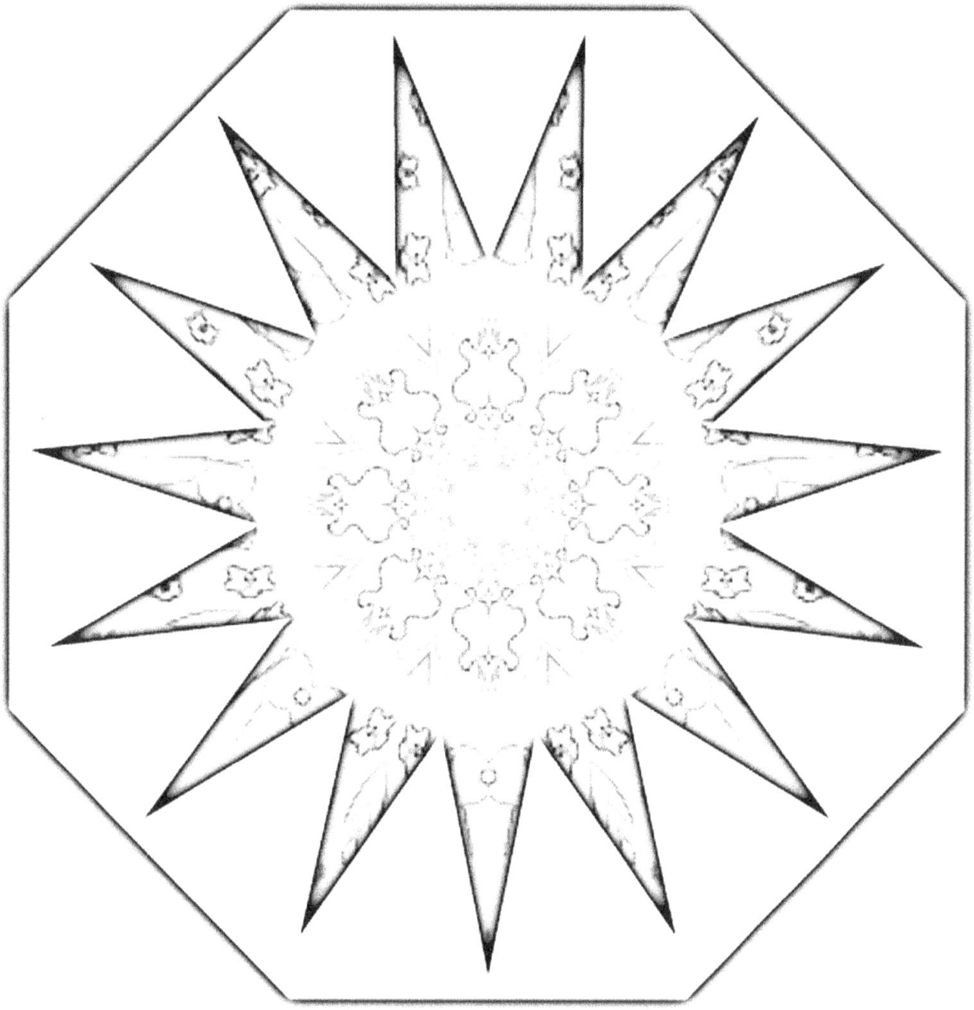

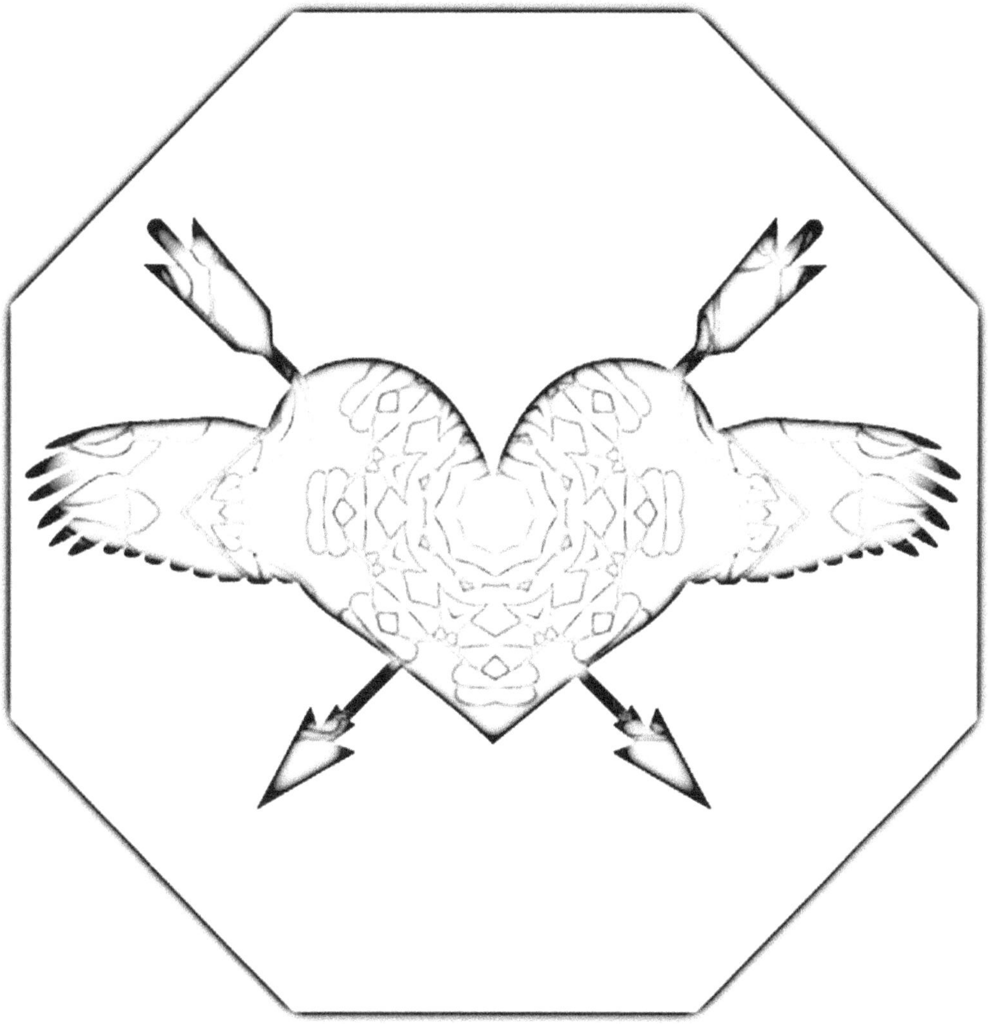

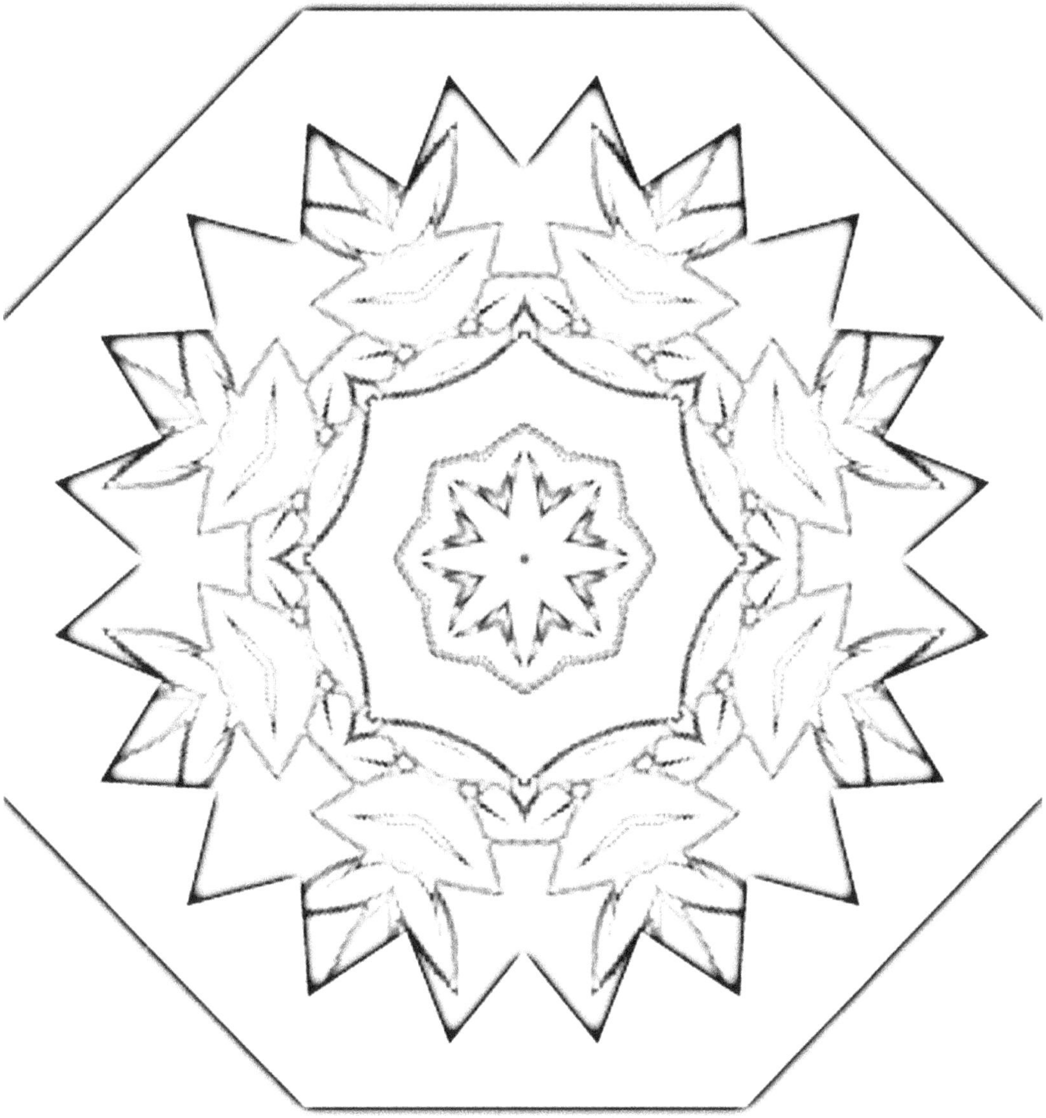

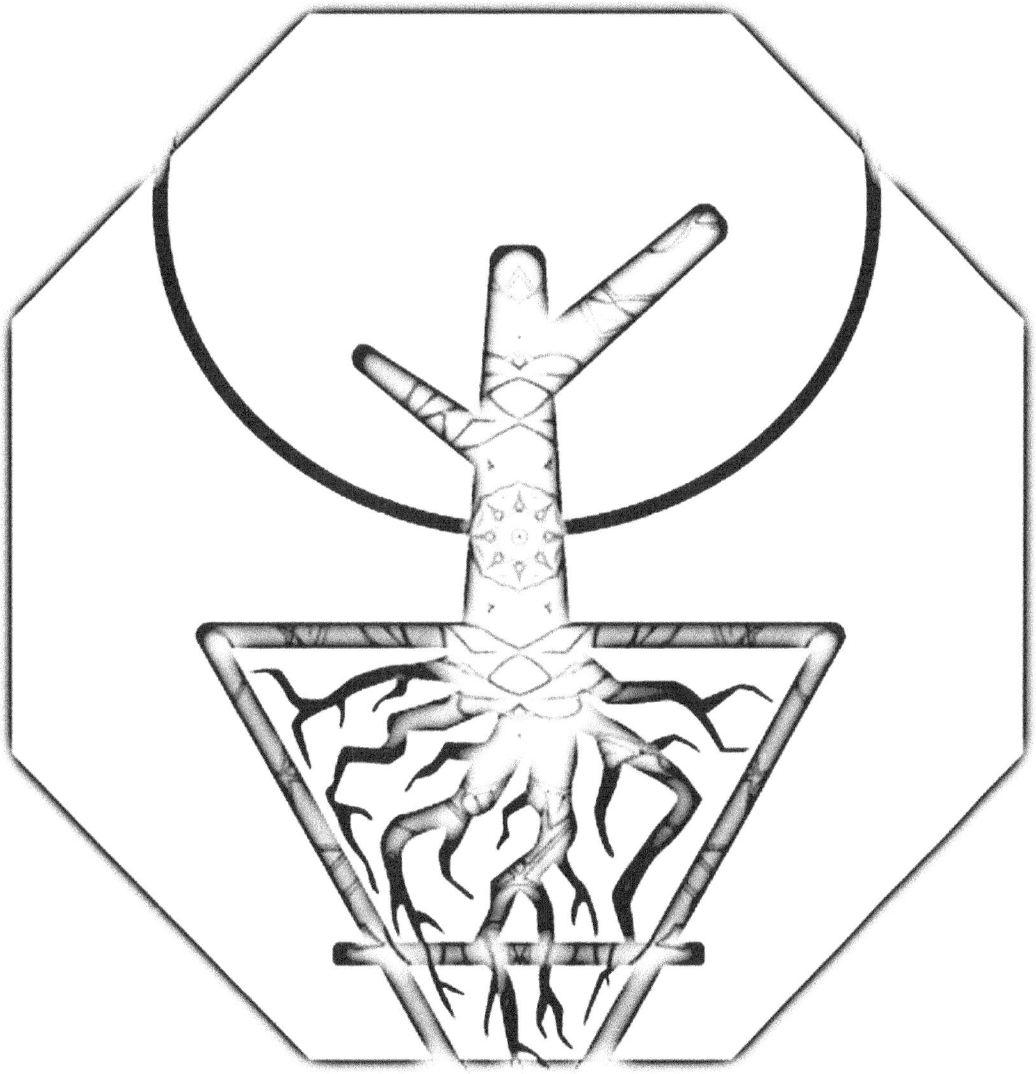

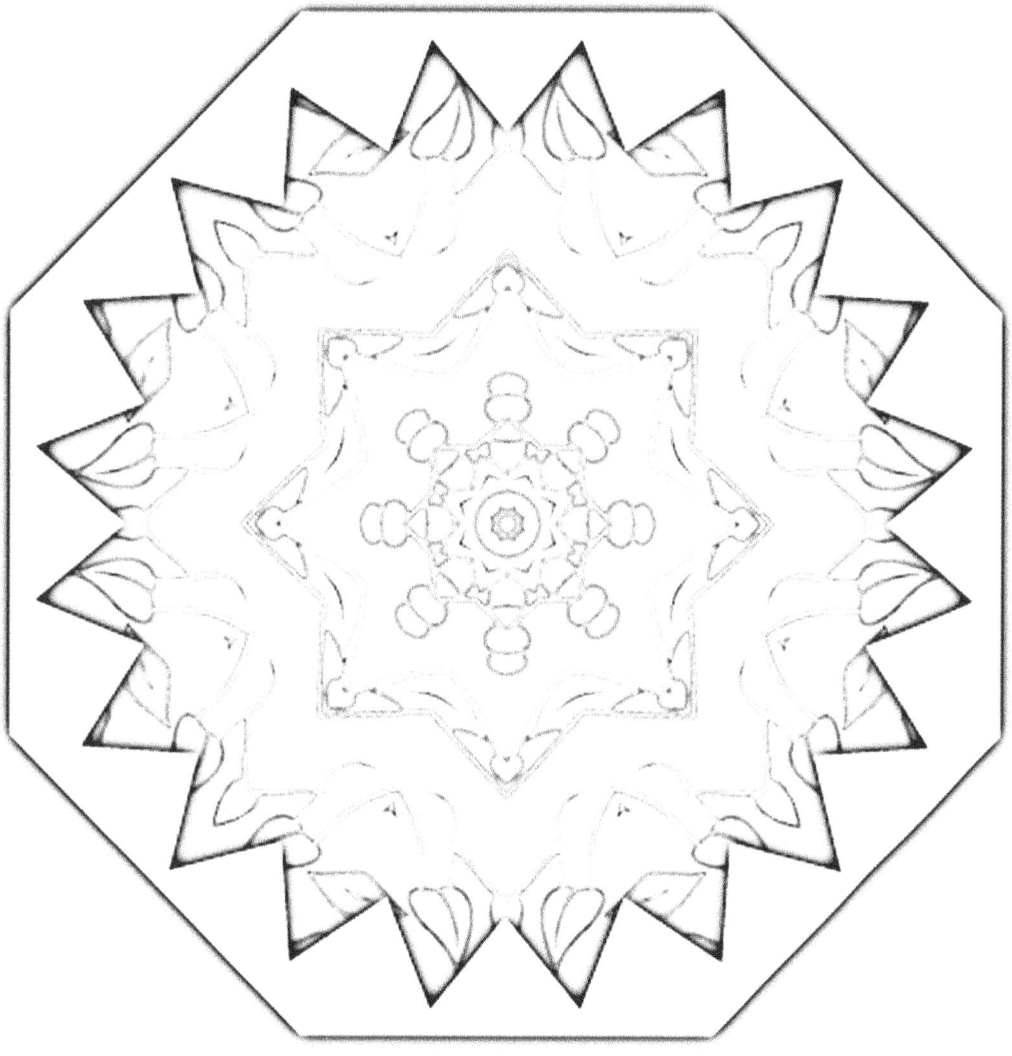

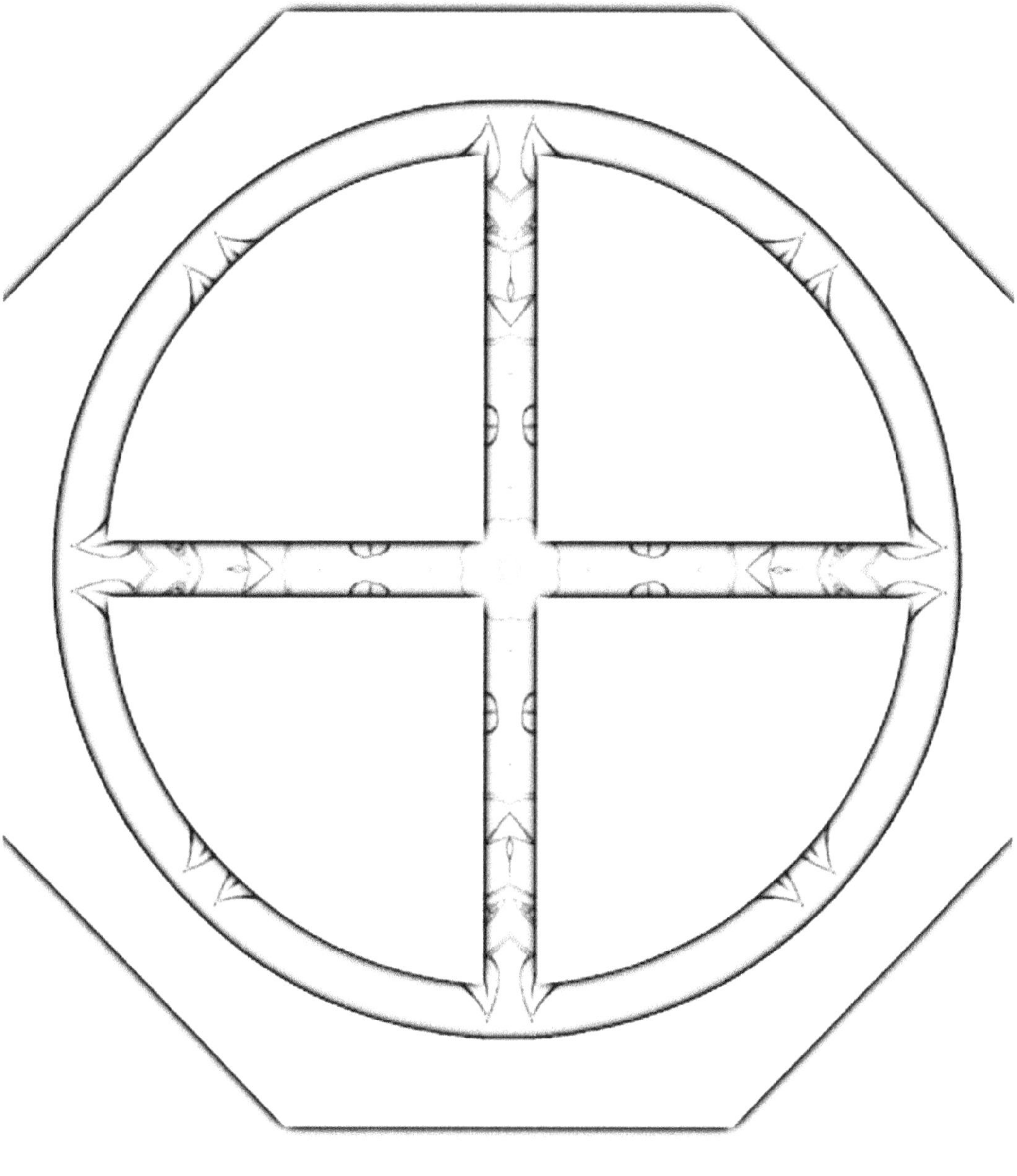

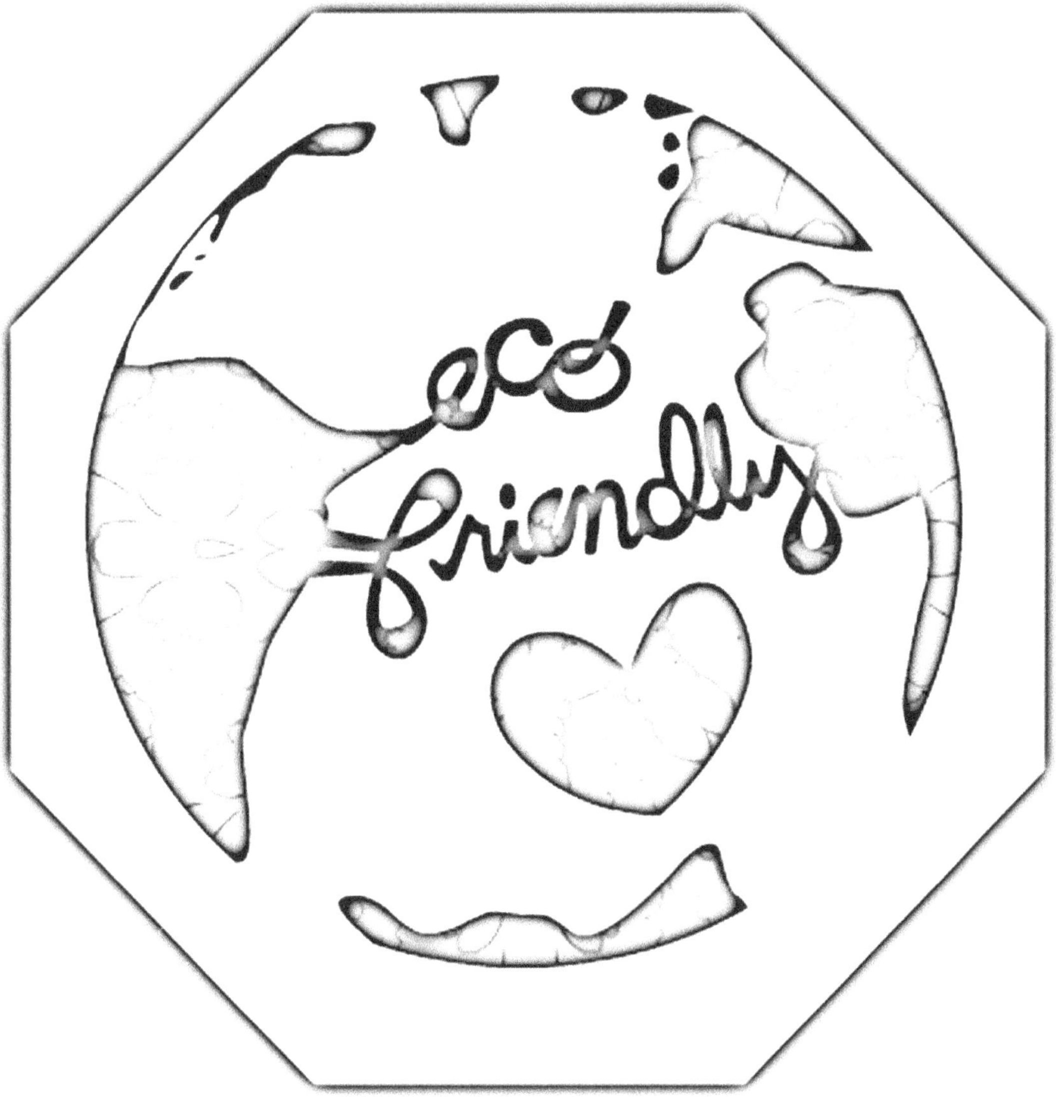
eco
friendly

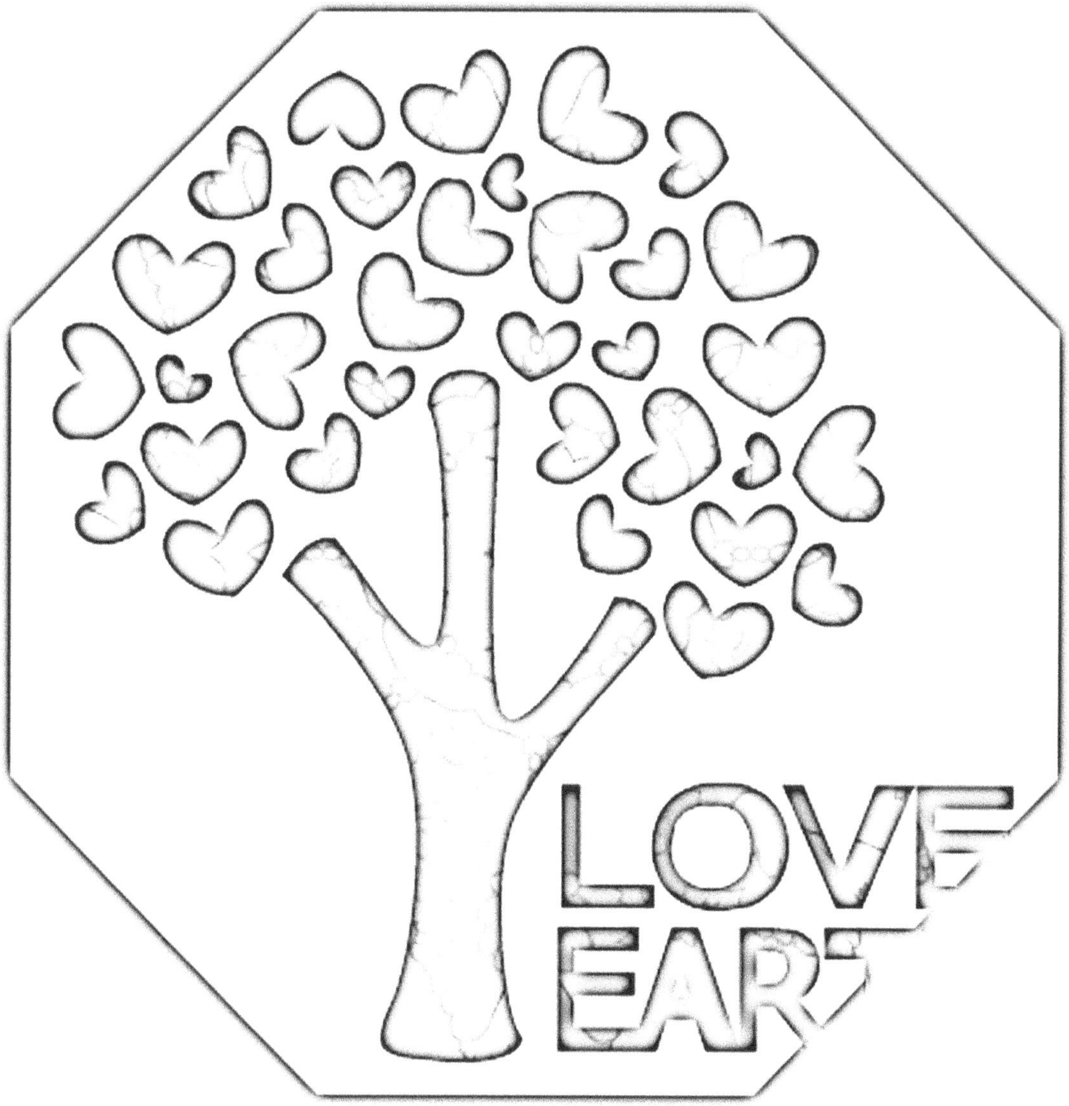
LOVE

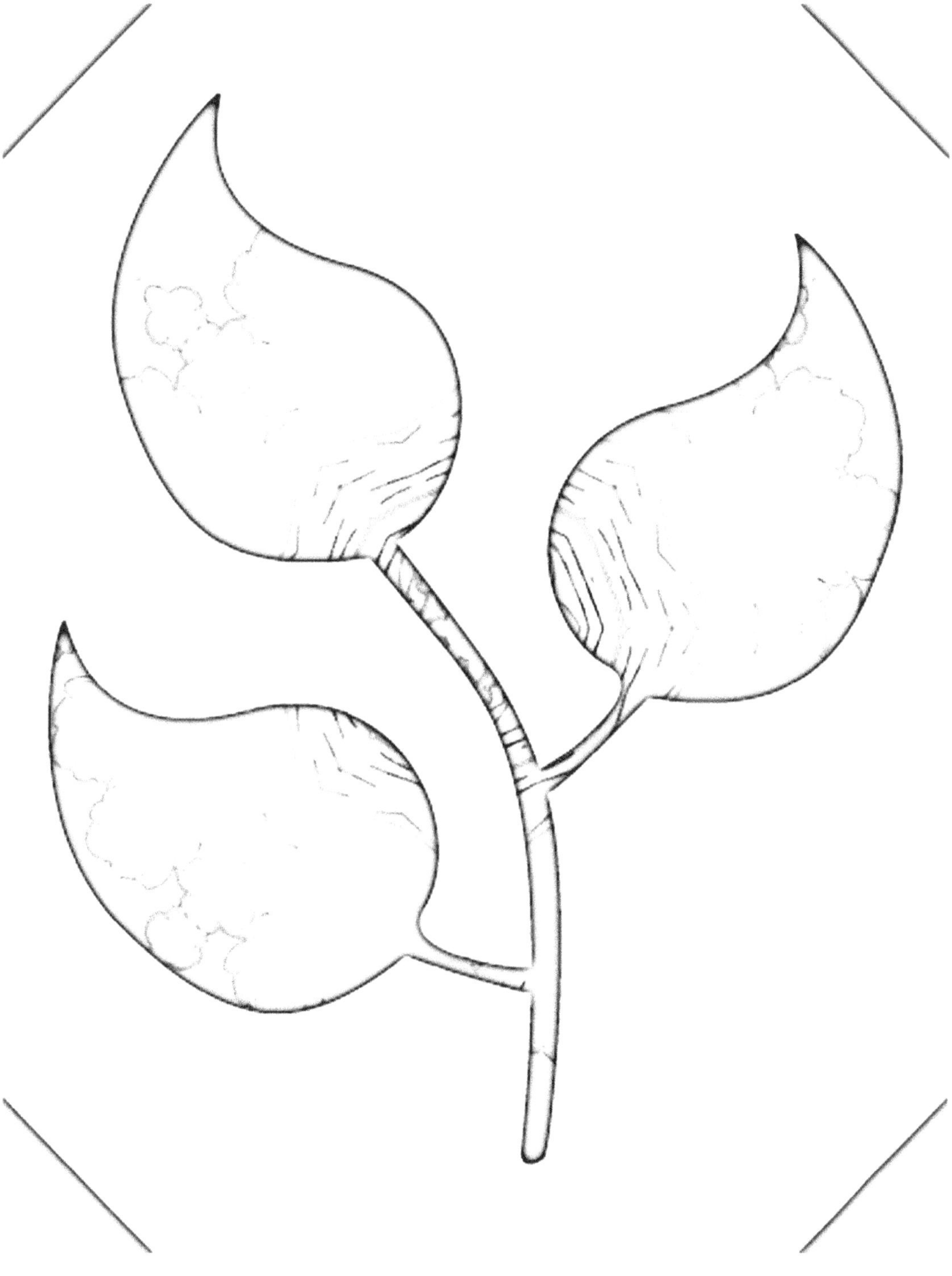

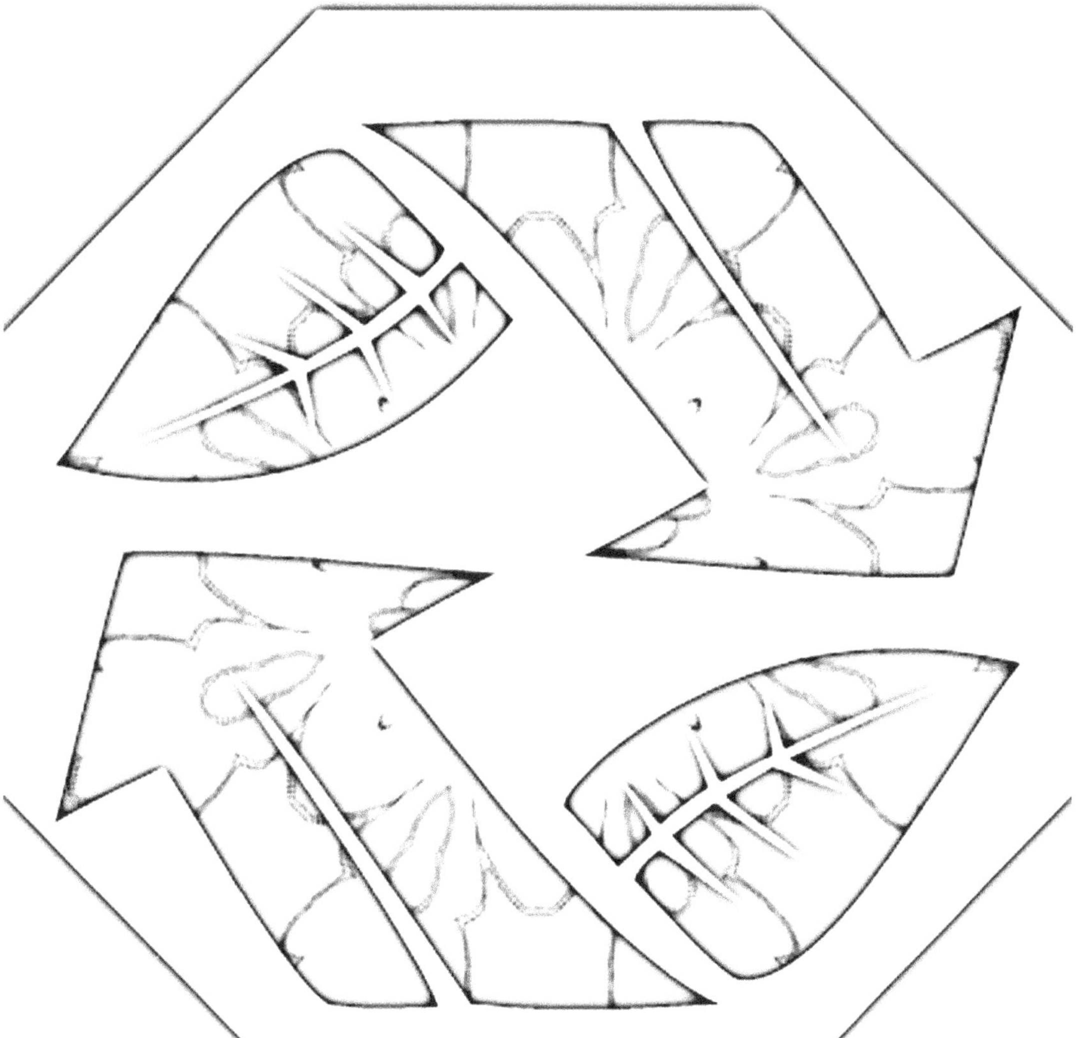

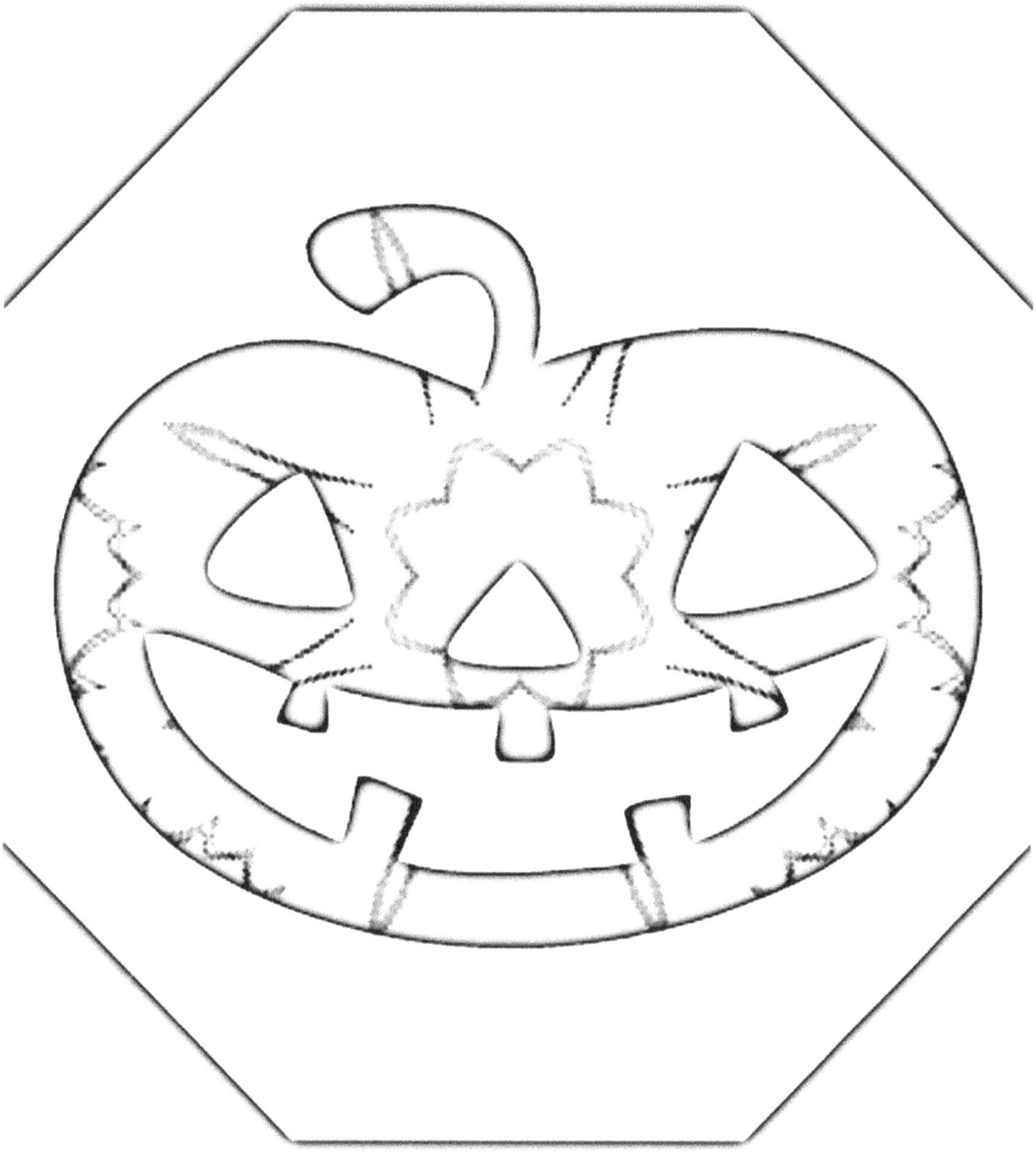

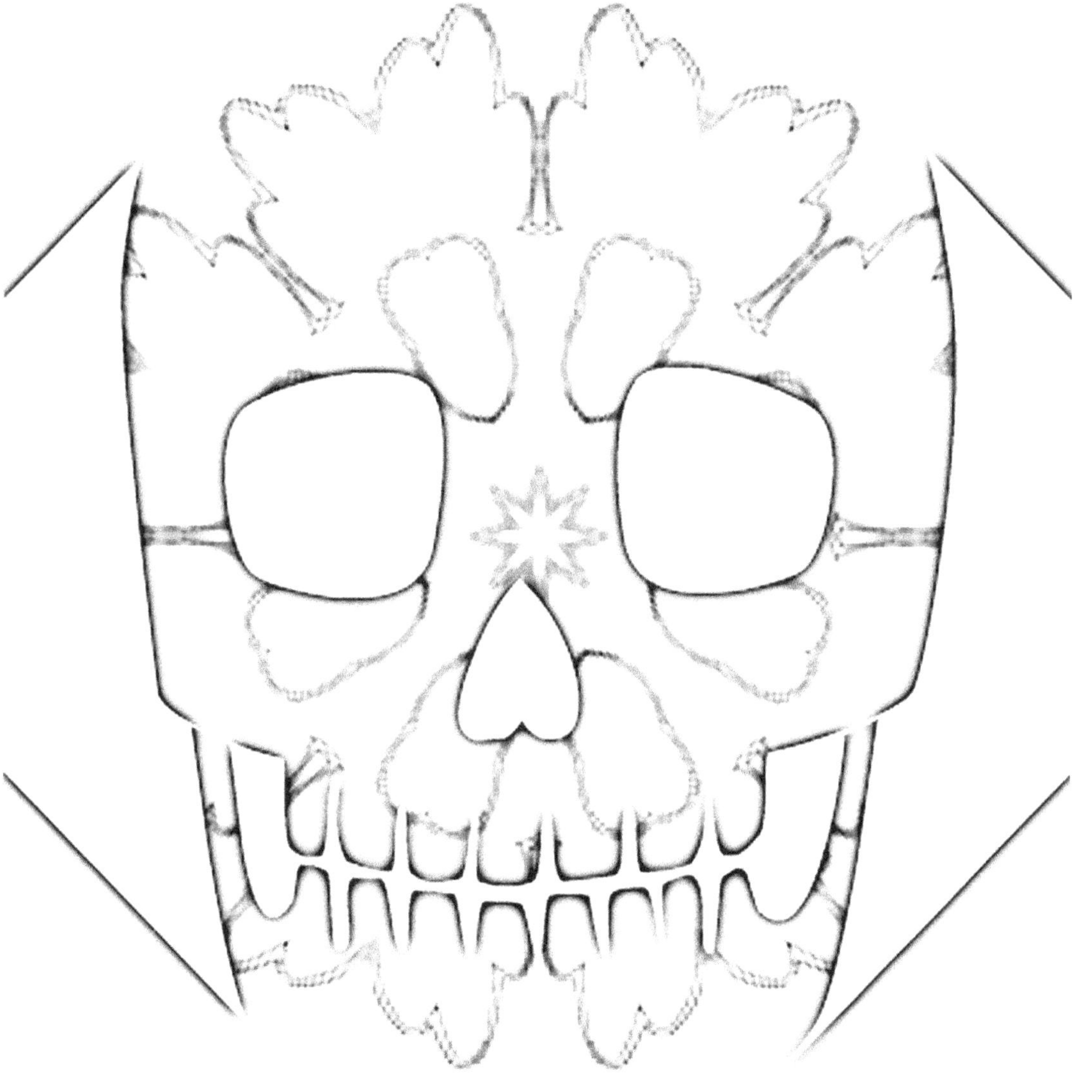

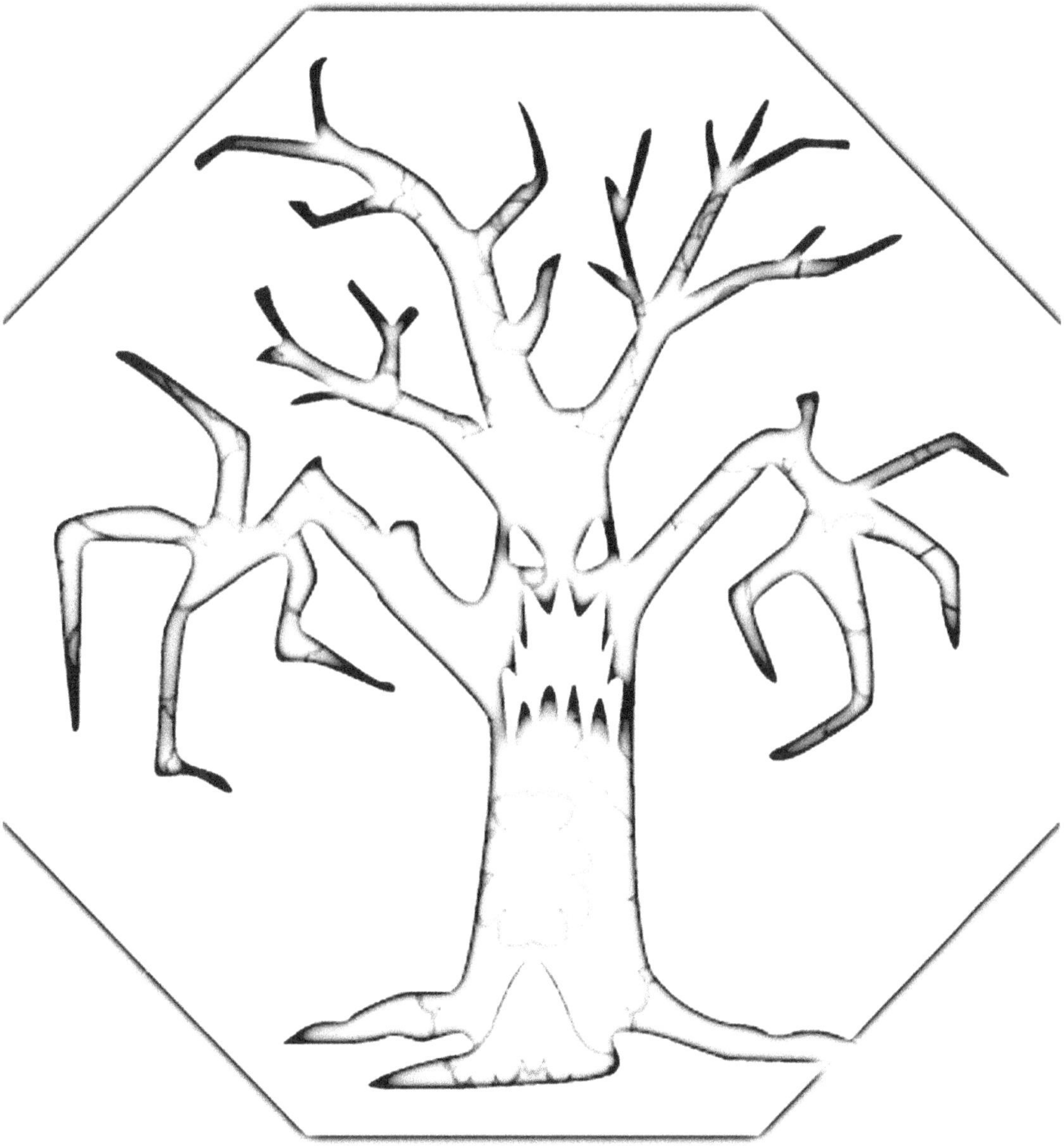

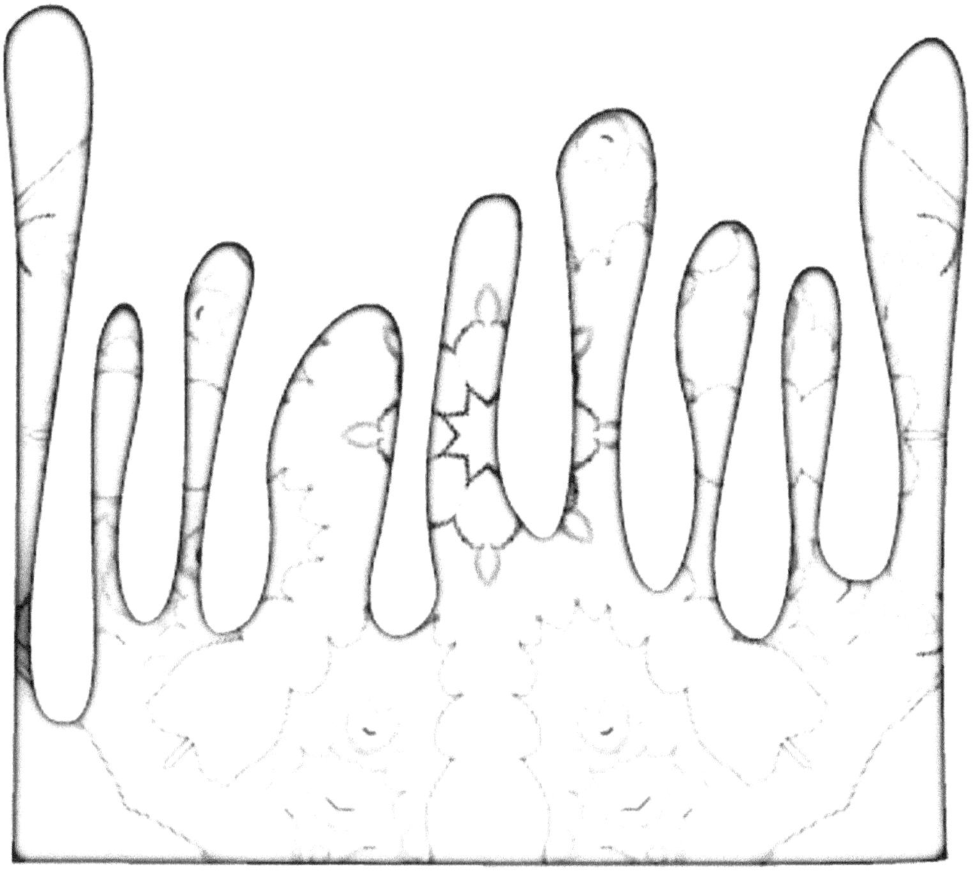

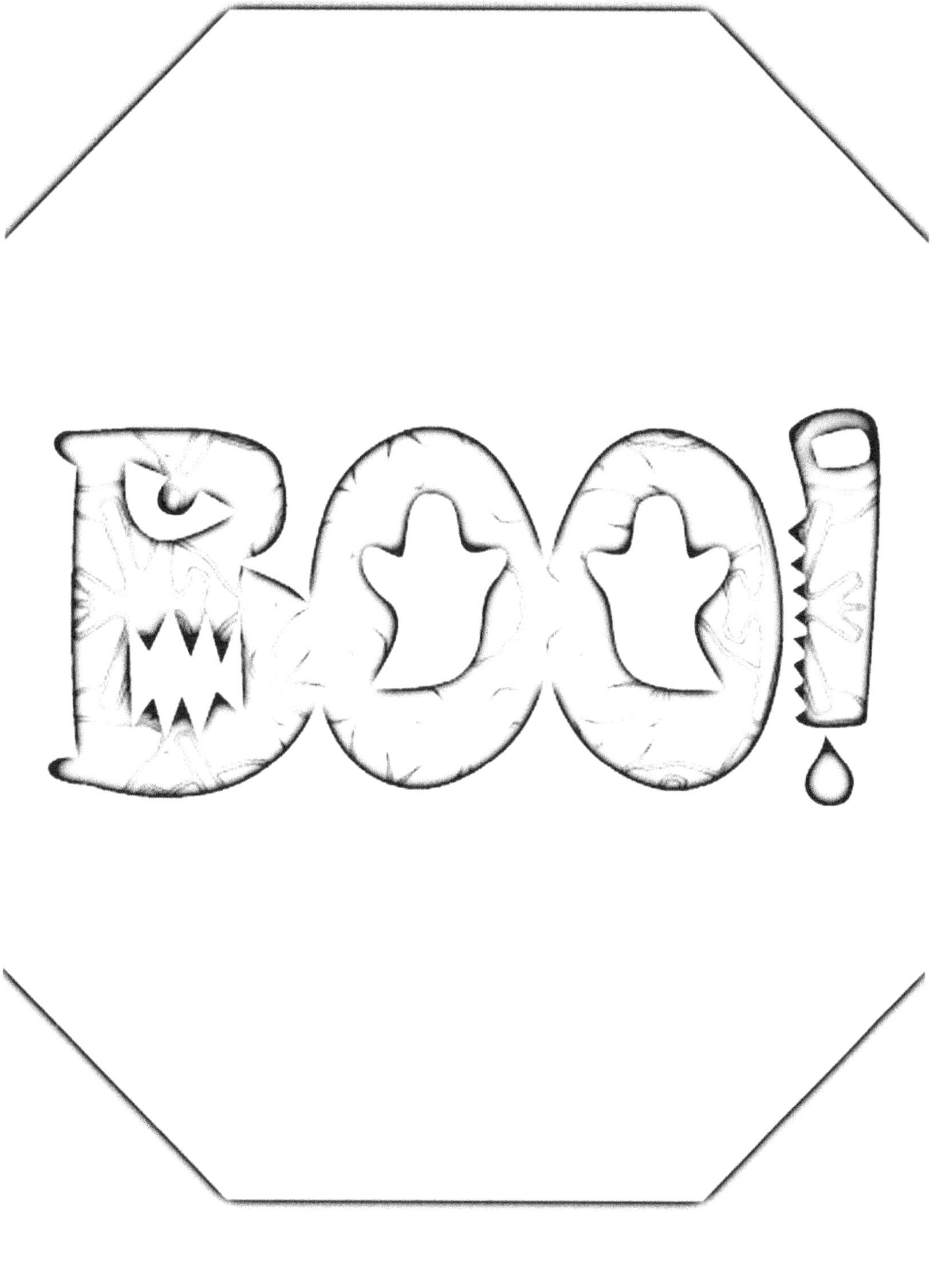
BOO!

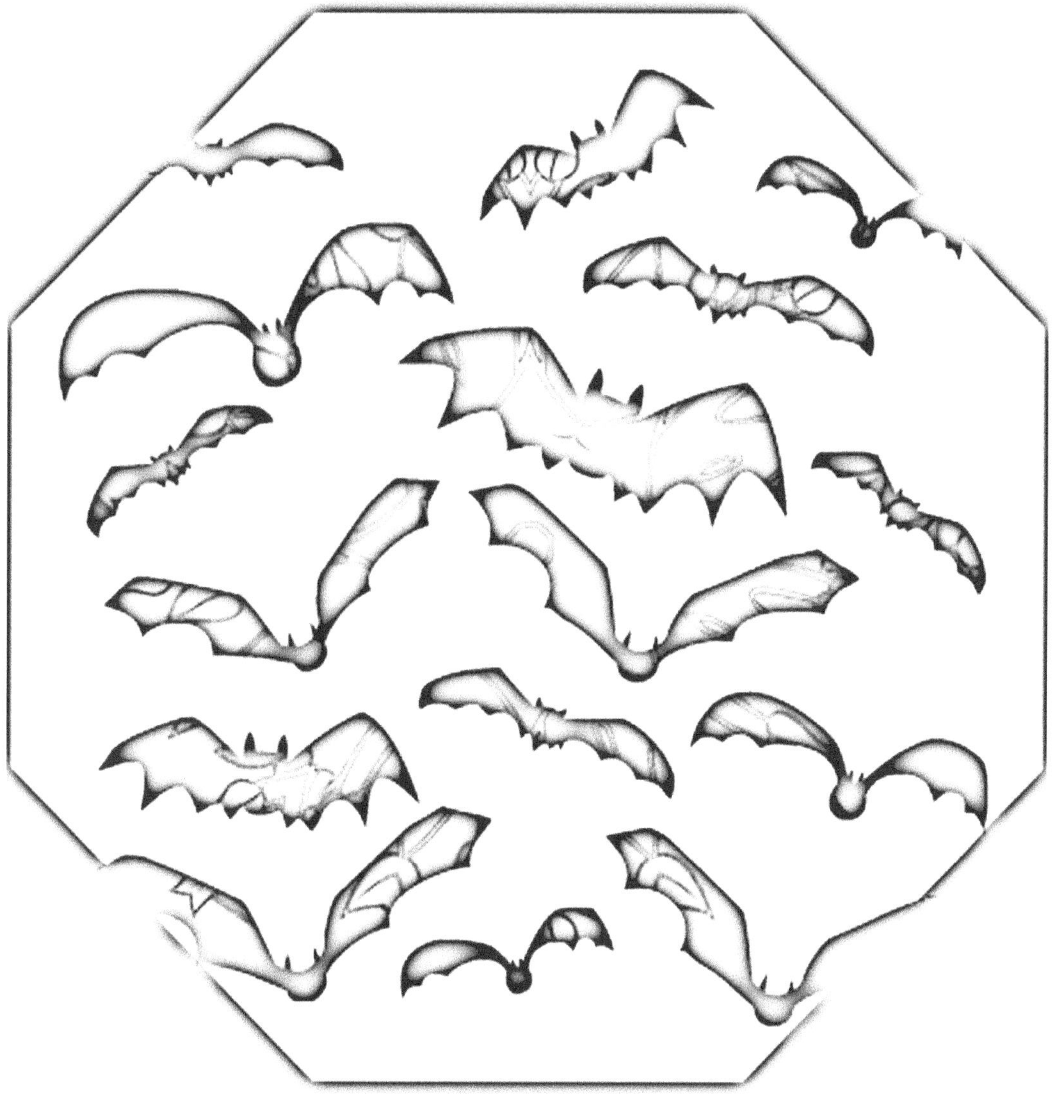

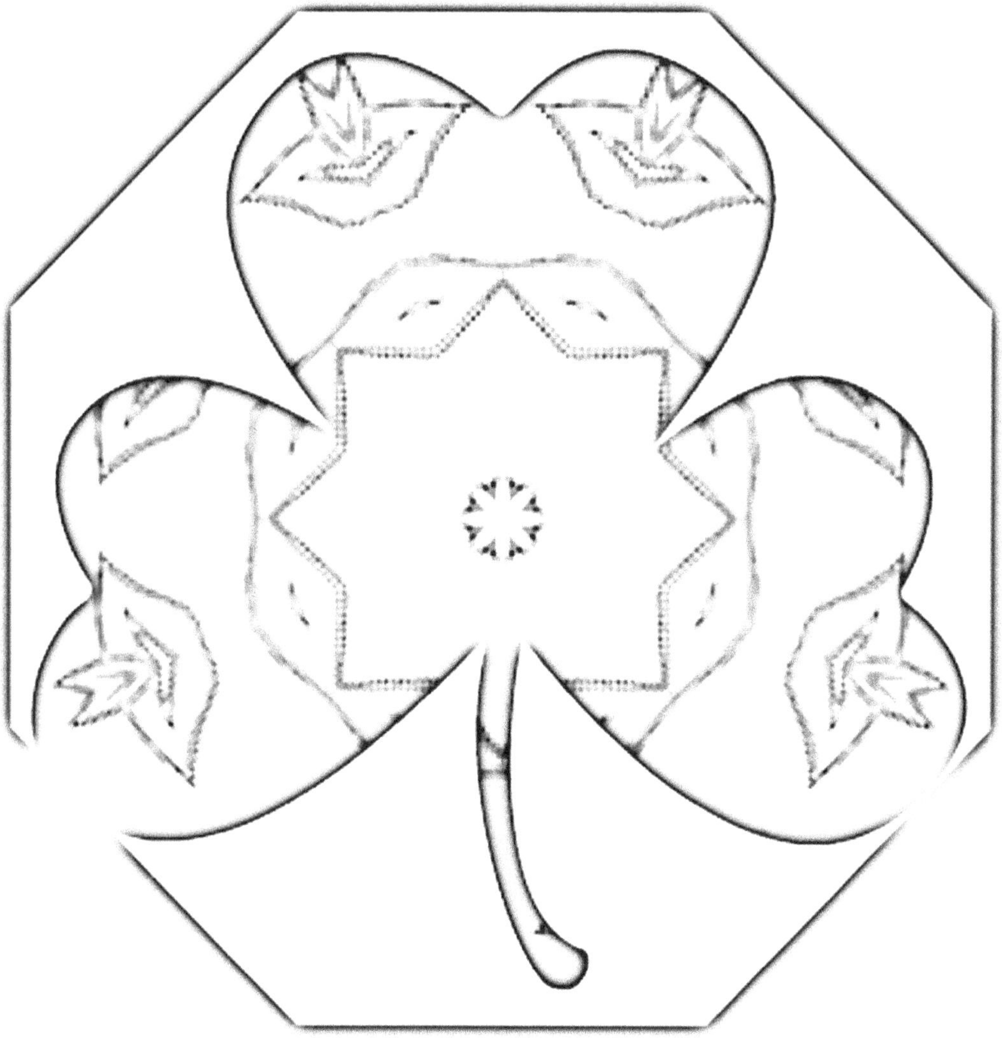

Note

www.ingramcontent.com/pod-product-compliance
Lightning Source LLC
Chambersburg PA
CBHW080651180526
45168CB00008B/3375
9781517597757